END ALL
& BE ALL

GREGG FRIEDBERG

END ALL & BE ALL

Three lyric cycles.

Each cycle, less or more disclosed story.

Each lyric, less or more composed worry.

Embajadoras Press
Ontario, Canada

GREGG FRIEDBERG lives in Ohio and Guanajuato.

He's happiest creating sequences of poems like those comprising *End All & Be All*: loosely, not conventionally narrative, a matrix of themes considered from an evolving perspective.

Other works by him:

Three Winter Disaffections along the Upper Sandusky, three poem sequences
What's Wrong? a lyrical fable
The Elopement, a lyrical diary
The Best Seat Not in the House, a sequence of poems
The Artist's Reception, a series of photos paired with texts
Would You Be Made Whole? a collection of unruly sonnets
Mr Godiva, a Shakespearean tale in five acts
Why We Polka, a play
Me Gustaría Decirte Algo / I'd Like to Tell You Something,
    poems with facing-page Spanish translations
    by Humberto Hernández Herrera

ISBN 978-1-988394-31-2

Embajadoras Press
Ontario

Copyright © 2024 by Gregg Friedberg

Cover: Italian coast, photo by Ken MacDonald

Thanks to Ken MacDonald

and to Bill Kierspel

CONTENTS

Acknowledgments

I   END ALL & BE ALL

Tiresias at Fiumicino (love among the ruins)	3
Late nude (the seismographer at fault)	7
Heavy sea (recollected in tranquility?)	8
Climb to the crater (false pregnancy)	10
Late nude (at the artist's reception)	12
Quit kiss (world without end)	13
The break with her and Peter's church (over the phone)	14
Late nude (the snapshooter in an attic window)	16
Wayside host (cross words)	17
On the prayer queue (what will happen when it rains?)	20
Late nude (suicide over Main Street)	23

II   GOSPEL

Patient he is in a land of frantic people	27
"You don't know me," I told him	27
Shifting scapes, the stagger of cedars acrest a ridge	28
He's never so light as in light's first flush	29
Mystery of the standing-butt circle	29
Lately I hear and sense and see extraordinarily	30
After his ordeal in the wilderness	31
At every station of the cross consider us	32

High on his crossbeam, planning his hard next move	33
Picture my switch hoisting the spirited sponge	34
His shadow crawls across the place of skulls	34
The collective fever: he begged it from us	35
With hide scraps I shod his feet	35
My love was like a middling rose	36
My hand rests on my still chest	37

III COFFEE AND TIRAMI SU?

"Coffee and tiramisù?"	42
My old love's new wife and I have dined alike	43
It begins with a crush on Benito	45
and check into the Afterlife	47
Then we'll read solely between the lines	48
Thin ice	50
Cleared, then set afresh	52

Index of titles / first lines — 55

About the author

Acknowledgements

Gospel, in an earlier version, appeared in the poetry journal **Assaracus**

END ALL & BE ALL   I

TIRESIAS AT FIUMICINO (love among the ruins)

Was it only yesterday
we were sitting on the hull
of a beached boat? feet bare

knees drawn up
trying God's love, the sand black
under the volcano.

You said He loves us but like
the volcano loves us
as occasions to redeem
and pushed up my blindfold.

Your hair was short and the sun setting.
The wind raised a fringe of it like a wing.

•

There are too few occasions for love,
you say, to miss one

among the ruins
alongside the windsocks
and shrimp nets.

And yet not we nor anyone, I think,
not love nor anything
is meant to be here

on these stump walls decayed past regret

past sweet but past bitter too
past take-off *and* landing.

•

If I say stop, you'll stop, won't you?
not force me?

It's not that I don't want it.
I do . . . deep inside.

But it might
prove too much for me.
It could.

Try, you say
and tug down my blindfold.

O God! I moan. Is *this* Your love?

Fantastic! you say. Like yesterday.
Don't resist. Take it.

Plague by famine.
Fire by drought.
Flood by quake.

O God! I plead, please don't make me.

•

You're still keeping yourself apart, you say,
still tight in yourself. God can't love you
that way. And you can't love His creation.
Let it ravish you!

Then it will seem like love? I ask.

Just like, you say.

Oh God, I say.

It's not a spike through the palm, you say. Take it.

Tick by tock.
Church by palace.
Street by block.

•

Up and over the sea into thin air.

They give us blankets and pillows
but you say we can't do it here.

That surprises me. If some truth
wants telling why deny it? prefer fiction
or a crossword.

I guess if you don't want me, though,
I'll move to an unoccupied row
lucky there is one.

I get stiff on these long flights, gas
if I'm not serviced,

cover my lap with a blanket
and my eyes after checking
no one can see.

•

On the ferry back from Vulcano
you met this blond boy exploring:

Make photo of me? asks he,
by this canoe of rescue?

He thinks you're not French.

You compose him in his little chamber.

He you in yours.

He you in his.

You him in yours.

There are too few occasions for love
to miss one between the lifeboats,
the traytables –

"Hard or soft liquor? which shall it be, sir?
Or would you rather miss?"

I calm down my blanket,
push up my blindfold.

Which *is* His love?

LATE NUDE (the seismographer at fault)

You uncapped your lens, zoomed in –
right off you recognized:

he's monitoring with faulty equipment!
Not a blip on the graph for *how* long?

He wants shaking up! at your hands
a good shaking!

Just shake his hand?
Would that make you complicit?

What is the mercy of the thing?

On the rift-sown boulders compose him.
Shoot, then re-pose him.

Did your hand shake? your visit shock?
Did it license the earth's aftershocks?

HEAVY SEA (recollected in tranquility?)

Listy table, creaky chair,
        peggy pencil, vacant square,
                dreggy cup – it won't help
                        refilling it but thanks for the offer.
                The neck massage neither and leave
        those right where they are, please.
I'll look to my own mess.

You mean well, I know,
        but it meant so much more
                when you steadied me naked
                        on the wobbly rocks leveed
                against a heavy sea, against
        the chillbrine, the crashsuck.
Then you stood back

and I stepped stormward.
        It growled and I groaned.
                It flogged and I spread for it.
                        It hung in my nostrils, I – o yes –
                its witness more than my own
        and my own more than now.
Where is that witness?

no sooner borne than flashed,
        clapped, cast away.
                Leave those, I say! Didn't you hear?
                      False starts are not for other eyes.
                Yours least of all I want
        to see me mounted –
splayed and pinned on dirty sheets,

or how, to mine a vein, I keep it
        bleeding, that I've betrayed you
                for a nifty turn of phrase.
                      Why let *you* see how
                  disappointment too inspires me?
      that whatever the nature,
I'll turn it into squalls on paper.

CLIMB TO THE CRATER (false pregnancy)

Sorry to say, you've lost our way, strayed
from the stamped, approved path
into a labyrinth of gullies!

I'm not *worried*. Up is up and down is down.
How wrong can we go?

And I *like* watching you sidewind, suck in
those sexy abs . . .

It comes upon you suddenly, doesn't it?
the conviction that you're lost.
After you've been for a while.

Consider the bud that seals your doom:
you don't recognize it.

It blooms: now you do.

The Great Tragedian works those strings, plays you
for the ladies and gentleman: cocky . . . aghast . . .
ruined.

They were watching when you missed the turn
that led them right to the top.

There's always *something* you're ignorant of, you know.
And then you're not:

the tick of the psychical clock
and the tock – watch your step! Gosh, it *is*
a big crater, isn't it?

Your lip's quivering . . .

I want to throw myself in, you think,
snuff any chance we'll go wrong.

Like yesterday in the fray of a heavy sea.

Well, it tempts you, doesn't it? such majesty:
"Break the bad habit of come-what-may.
End all and be all."

So long as you play hard to get
it leers and leers at you.

The others have started down – our turn
to be superior!

If you blind an eye
you'll make out Cyclops hiding in ambush.

Blind both
and you'll fathom Vulcan's gorge rising . . .

Better not! you quickened and swelled my belly
with barely a wink.

I feel the pull and you feel I'm bound
to let go, slip out of your fate,

gloat over all the quakes that can never shake me,
all the eruptions I'll miss,

blow old Aeschylus
a teasing kiss.

LATE NUDE (at the artist's reception)

Among these portraits I made of him
he went dressed all in blue. Disguised as sky?

A dream? A friend
took it as a tease. The wine
ripened her resolve.

"These are nudes that keep a secret."
That's the gauntlet she threw down
and then took aim:

"It's only fair that *he* expose it!"

He lifted a shoe, loosed
the lace – those too were blue! – left them
up to her.

She bared his foot, then *de*posed it,
slipped the other knot. Others noticed,
turned to watch.

He canvassed our eyes,
took charge of his unveiling, and nude,
his place: last in the series, faced

the hush

that met the marks of his disease.
My trained eye marked his shivering hand.

Hers reached for mine, and so again
this afternoon, paying our respects.

QUIT KISS (world without end)

Something has to be your first memory.

But what if you're told it's best forgotten?
Accept the revised standard version instead.

And something revealed to you
that hardest fact of life:

invest, invest – and then you're divested!
The dark at the end of the tunnel.

And something, the next hardest: shame, I mean.
The great shocks of getting the self into focus.

You blinker your eyes to keep going, master a tease
involving asses and pussies and cocks!

Weird, you think, but you learn the moves,
veil the zoo below your belt.

World *without* shame? without end? – what would it be like?
Blue Boy without blue? Or only blue?

Mustn't linger over those lips: a quick, quit kiss,
then pull the sheet up over the head.

They're so frail, the ones we're invested in.
You're either grieving or blushing on account of them.

If you remember something, how acquiesce
in the demand that you don't?

And if you don't, in the gospel that you do?

THE BREAK WITH HER AND PETER'S CHURCH (over the phone)

I know: I'm the one always says
what people *say* doesn't matter.

Think of it as noise. Turn a deaf ear.
But a keen eye. I mean,
to discover if you love someone.

Even so: a *little* progress in the conversational arts . . . tact.
No, more than that: dignity – *there*'s the word.
I don't *think* I'm contradicting myself.

I'd been saying how once you've sieved off the rhetoric,
the Reformation's all about stripping away everything
that obscures God's will.

When is our nature most carnal?
when we're young? or old?

It's between we've got the best shot
at dignity.

Right, you want to get a little stored up
with the years.

No, not much point in criticizing a person
for her very nature. Or a church for that matter.
But after ten years . . .

You think it odd to love someone then stop
loving them?
If you put it that way.

But it's a matter of distance. How can you be together
if you've grown apart?
I've gone on ahead.

She didn't take it well. I doubt she'll call again.
She didn't actually say that.
She didn't say anything.

I didn't want to say any more. *I*'d said my piece.

I had no idea it was going to happen. Having it out, I mean.
That's not the right way to put it, is it?

It just got to me. The perversity of it.
You think she'll get in touch, do you?

After a little time goes by? a little healing time.

You really do? Maybe grow a little on account of it.

It's on account of it being my birthday she phoned.
I don't know how we got onto the Reformation.

I think I said something about how we seem wise –
when we do – only in what remains obscure,
in those places clarity hasn't yet claimed.

Silence.
Neither of us saying anything.

I think it would have been all right except
it was over the phone.
Turn a deaf ear – what's left?

God's will, I guess.

LATE NUDE (the snapshooter in an attic window)

Slivers of glass shiver over his head.
Smoke gushes through a gash in the roof.

What in the flaming hell is he thinking?

He's thinking:

> "Everyone's out on the sidewalks, pointing
> fingers, clucking tongues, sirens wailing.
>
> Simple folk though curators of substantial
> collections. *Cave incendium!*
>
> After three months' drought the sisal doormats
> have grown down to the street curbs.
>
> I'm composing one portly burgher
> in my little chamber –
>
> don't he look fishy?
> Look at his lips wriggle!
>
> He has one, too! My ears are burning!
> This is so cool, maneuvering each other
>
> in each other's! Why, my hands are shaking!"

Why they're shaking:

A ladder's coaxing his elbows.

Shout up to him? mind him
of the moment
of the moment?

WAYSIDE HOST (cross words)

I'll wager they bake once a week – at most,
        resurrect the freshness in the microwave.
Once those pans did nightly service
        like the ones in the museum case.

Vesuvius the last to heat them up, you say,
        make a face and spit into your palm.
Bits of lamb in that one? Sorry. Not that one too?
        Fishy. More's the pity.

Thou shalt not partake of God's ferociousness
        but of a chocolate kiss.
A choice of the sort called moral,
        the sort that makes us human.

You nod to mean I've got that right.
        To be sure, I'll multiply it for you
else you'll certainly go hungry. A tough position,
        the human one, hence our shorter

shelf-life – reduced by a factor of, what, thirteen?
        since our sore-abused first dad.
Baked goods' extended sevenfold meanwhile.
        Why not let's put in here?

finish these beneath Jesus' agony.
        All picnic spots, you say,
should be redeemed this way – better:
        ban the bloody baskets absolutely!

You want us extended too, you and me.
        What good other longevities if we're cut short?
our love gone stale? You can't bear the thought
        of our love gone stale.

The French use *préservatifs*. But yours is a hard case –
       you're hard to draw out. Do you really want
to last and last, laid out on oil cloth
       marked down for quick sale?

By the way, a scientist has demonstrated fish feel pain.
       You glare at me in profile as if to say: fish *too*?
and just who *hadn't* known in his *clean* breast?
       though they can't give voice to it.

But you have the vocation, I'm convinced,
       you've heard the call.
I know some things, you say, I do,
       important things.

It's when it comes to you unsought –
       yea, unwanted – that you trust in it.
Dragged to more respectable
       than *panting after*.

No substitute for experience, though,
       so would I please make you one?
for the wall behind your work table?
       Passion-sized.

Leave Jesus out of it: loops to slip *your*
       limbs through
so you can tell what needs to be
       from that vantage.

If truth be told, you're not certain
       I want to hear! No need for Pharisees
or Romans, just a step stool and a hook
       for the telephone.

You'll say: "No more suffering for His sins!"?
       You're contradicting yourself,
aren't you? - you're crying, aren't you?
       Let me see.

"He called us separate out of the void, but not
       separate enough: composed in one
belly, decomposed in another – *that's*
       original sin," you sob, "– stop poking me!"

and shake and hold your head. "He claims
       all the credit, deserves the blame."
But if *Jesus* tried to save His face and failed?
       "The call comes in, you take it,

set the pan of yourself in the pyroclastic flow."
       Kiss?
Close your eyes. Try the taste.
       Vinegar.

ON THE PRAYER QUEUE
(what will happen when it rains?)

Hello?
      Hello?

I phoned earlier. Left a message then too.
I guess you haven't got it yet.

I phoned her too.
Left a message.

Haven't heard back yet.
It's been all of five minutes!

I can't help worrying.
They're so frail, the ones we're invested in.

You don't need *me* to tell *you* that!

Last night I dreamt:
one of your angels appeared unto her

and bade her plaster her house with dung – oh,
need I tell you? a hailstorm worthy

of your old testament knocked
the old siding off. Like the sky'd fallen.

A shame having to deal with that now,
she being so sick, and no money for repairs.

She was lounging topless in the backyard. Gorgeous –
in my dream, I mean.

A mixed drink in one hand
and in her lap *The Decline of the West.*

She asked, "What will happen when it rains?"

Now the sky was clear to the horizon,
far beyond as the angel knew, and he grew impatient:

"Whole villages in India are shit-faced.
And it's common practice in Arkansas.

Dar'st thou doubt the wisdom of the Lord,
the Omniscient Father Who created thee? . . . "

Those epithets!
I surprised myself I could script the angel so handily.

But then dark clouds gathered,
and the angel changed into Martha Graham!

Satin to sackcloth. Wings into elbows.
That happens in dreams, that sort of thing.

I was phoning to offer my help.
With making arrangements, at least.

Money, if she'll accept it.
I doubt she will.

But I could only leave a message.
Asking her to phone me back.

It's been all of five minutes – eight or nine.
I know, I'm tying up the line.

What if it was a wrong number?! I left my message
for a stranger!

Will he take pity on me? phone me back
and set me straight . . .

Please return my call.

LATE NUDE (the suicide over Main Street)

En pointe, silhouetted against the rooflines,
she had all your attention, your camera's
eye.

But look, you hadn't noticed: a figure
in a cross-paned window.

He adds pity and you dare to think:
chef d'oeuvre – Oh damn!

DAMN!

You've done this before: the valedictorian
flanked by the head and tail of

GO OD LUCK!

There's a weathervane pricking her privates!

Why not (you kick yourself) just make it a rule?
a quick check all around before springing
the shutter!

How much coast is there to guard?

How much coast *is* there to guard?

GOSPEL II

GOSPEL

Patient he is
in a land of frantic people.

In the shade. In full sun.
Failing no less than prevailing.

Patient with me.
And without.

•

"You don't know me," I told him
one day after intimacy.

"But I know you because however I
conceive you is how you are."

Although what I think I want
isn't what I really want, is it?

After so many trials, as many errors
we've figured that out.

He's at my window, forlorn, as if
a glass pane could keep us apart.

Or in a bar booth, petting a girl as if
he fancied her.

So he pays for my sins,
over and again.

The guiltier my accusing finger,
the more he owes.

•

Shifting scapes, the stagger
of cedars acrest a ridge . . . these

stirred my torpid sense of things, disclosed me
closed down upon myself.

He took the stage. His words
unnerved me – his eye as he palavered them.

On God's right side:
the wrong side of remedy.

So now I'm convinced anew
of the enormity of things,

that intimacy's 'trick' candor,
close down upon myself again.

•

He's never so light
as in light's first flush.

It fancies him, but then *I*
plainly stare.

A delicious instant
that by insistence I debase.

It *is* my fault. He's
no more to blame

than any other
exhilarator of my soul.

I adore him on the wing
but would keep him in a cage,

by my gross and clumsy need reduced
to a flightless thing.

Why must he be mine
when he could just be?

●

A neat ring: butts poked
into the sand –

one, ash-end up,
live.

Has he been here? watching over
me?

Was it he and not the sun like hornets
waked me?

This aftertaste – is it him
in my mouth?

Shade the eyes: nothing
breaks the horizon line.

Dreams detain their personnel
at that strait gate to the undreamed place.

Mystery of the standing-butt circle.

●

Lately I hear and sense and see
extraordinarily:

his privacy through drawn curtains,
behind closed doors,

and scrupulously
record it all.

In time no one will know him
except by my account,

millions will know him
in detail so real and raw

by contrast all other notoriety
will seem crude caricature.

Were he to want me to,
I'd swear to keep his secrets.

Were he to appoint me
his biographer,

I'd write
not a word.

•

After his ordeal
in the wilderness –

distempered by day,
tempted by night –

pagan highwaymen seized him,
prodded him with pikes

all the way
to their capital,

sold him
to the temple priests.

No more wise words nor
compassionate ones,

no words at all, rather
shrieks and hisses,

baring of teeth, loping
from plinth to tablature,

ass high
and balls swinging.

"Shameless," they call him
in their foreign tongue.

•

At every station of the cross
consider us:

me transfixed
while he struggles, panting,

trailing blood
and sweat,

indulges
each grueling moment, bets

an unpledged future
on a terrific prank.

For a girl's astonishment?
Deplorable!

But will it prove
adorable?

I fear coward's fear,
scheme to halt

his halting progress
to no effect and yet for him –

were I asked
(he'll never ask) –

I'd madly give myself,
what's mine.

•

High on his crossbeam,
planning his hard next move . . .

His eye flares its surface,
this make-shift tower,

as if gravity were a delight
to tease!

I swear he grinned
ear-to-ear

even while
his earnest eye bled tears.

•

Picture my switch
hoisting the spirited sponge,

drizzling his cracked lips,
swabbing his sores . . .

my pen jotting notes:

" . . . *the bruised peach pleading
its succulence . . .*"

Someday we'll savor,
not mock him.

•

His shadow crawls
across the place of skulls.

•

The collective fever:

he begged it from us.
It consumed him.

Exhaust streams into space,
incandesces . . .

Holy smoke?

No deluded regicide,
no vain suicide, but cosmic sacrifice.

What are the odds against
that least assayable claim?

•

With hide scraps
I shod his feet

so they launched him surely,
nimbly.

Now his dead head hangs
between worlds.

The parted lips
of his wounds reveal

quivering tongues that jabber
hope, gibber dreams.

When I tow him along the highway,
most will look down.

A few
will stare.

He'll lose his hue, robins
will nest on his ledges

and hornets
beneath his overhangs.

•

My love was like a middling rose.
Like yours, I suppose.

Now he's a carrion flower.

Everyone comes to an end. How kin
to knowing that

is this end he's come to?

Like those neat circles
that band a globe: a conceit

corrupted by the real terrain.

All blithe spirit,
for its respect,

relies on time's opacity.

•

My hand rests
on my still chest.

The curtain flares
and shivers.

Beside the window a man
beguiled by my book

whittles a boy
on a cross.

The boy draws breath
then sags, innocent

of his caption, how
I scripted the carving knife.

III

COFFEE AND TIRAMI SU?

Cleveland. February.

*The speaker and his new partner
are in town for an evening performance
of all six Bartók string quartets – a rare treat
and they're excited.*

*They've spent the afternoon with the speaker's first love
and his new wife, meeting at the art museum, later
at a restaurant, weather worsening such that now
the two couples are the lone diners.*

"COFFEE AND TIRAMISÙ?"

The waiter's sweet tease
perks up the velveteen salon.

We're the last here.
Starched-bright linen's lip-
smirched.

He'd rather close up and go.
If only it weren't for *us*:

stage empty,
the cluttered set cleared
then set afresh.

Signore, lead us not into temptation
but if you do, then drive us not out.

MY OLD LOVE'S NEW WIFE AND I
HAVE DINED ALIKE

His late mother refused to attend the wedding.
Mixed marriage. Couldn't approve.

"It broke Mom's heart," he told me
while we stood in the lee of the Buddha's serenity.

"Dad's heartbroken now," husbands
the meals she made for him, then froze.

"I call them 'last suppers,'" he said, grinned,
watched himself blur in my eyes.

Strange creatures:

*need to see our face
and know the future but can do neither, and anyway
couldn't bear to, make do with fortune cookies
and our navel.*

We strolled away from Asian arts over
to photography: between-two-wars in black and white.

Then, you can tell, was fun.

Nowadays my love for him's
of a different sort.

Then why – or is that why, old boy,

that tear slipped down my cheek?

*why I faltered in mid-sentence, embarrassing myself,
pictured myself embracing you or, rebuffed,
chasing you*

*through the fragrant Marshall Field's,
on to the soda fountain?*

IT BEGINS WITH A CRUSH

on Benito
(he's just topped up your cup),

or Evita
(your cup toppleth over),

yes, ends with a crash,
with a crunch,

our head in a wicker basket, on a silver salver,
cock in a lobster's claw.

*Oh! those old ph'landery masters
of s&m nether lands!*

Santa's just an anagram of Satan,
the disguise so thin there's no excusing us:
gulled, queued on death row.

*First a blind eye . . .
then the vacant stare . . .*

The pendulum's dependabler careering
between elusive extremes
than sitting for our still-life portrait.

Nor can we be in the picture and outside it, too.
There's no violence violent enough
to work that subtlety!

*Unless, of course, it's all in sport –
a time out of deadearnest time:*

*have fun, and when you're done with fun,
slip off the playing field*

AND CHECK INTO THE AFTERLIFE

The downtown hotel shall be our resting place,
my new love's and mine.

On earth as it is in Heaven.

Pearly light, the piano's programmed cheer
prep us and we chart our symptoms,
diagnose our own anemic extravagance.

Disease we prefer to the cure.

Aren't there many such? Picture us,
after dinner, a smart smarting by Bartók,
returning for the petite mort.

My new love pockets the key.

Those keys unfingered depress and depress.

THEN WE'LL READ SOLELY BETWEEN THE LINES

"Dementia's far commoner than once supposed."

That's my old love's young love
minting after-dinner conversation.

A *scattered* brain's less daunting –
even an *absent* mind!

*The metaphors of ignorance. Of error.
In fact, the concert has begun.*

*The longing strains of the first movement
of the first quartet strain,*
  s   t   r   a   i   n . . .
strain . . .

wherefrom solace.

How is such alchemy possible?

However, we're absent: my new love's
misminded the starting time.

Oh! *this proves – does it not? –
not-knowing / knowing
are the flip / flop states of time,*

the tick and tock of creature mechanics,

and the transition:
quake, riot, all-up-for-grabs!

In the sudden throes of *dis*concertedness
we'll strain against the no-admittance door

while the fourth movement of number four
is plucked away from us,

the *un*blunted whips and whaps,
smarters of lucky souls not barred by brambles
in the brain.

My new love consults his watch,
sets down his cup.

Our time, he tells, is up.

THIN ICE

As we bundl'up cramp'dly in the vestibule,
he asks where we should breakfast.

Then I linger, prolong the goodbye.

"Enjoy the Bartók," my old love cheers.
An encore embrace, breaths of licorice.

He knows, of course, through all the years *he*
disappointed me, Bartók never did.

Do we live, do you think, in bedeviled times?
an accursed place, a riddled one?

supplied with oracles, forewarned of what's –
or not – to come?

what we're in for, what we're not,
whether wished for or against?

Why not take a minute? check
it's not your dad you're slewing,
not your mom you're screwing,

decrypt the odd character
on your birth-slash-death certificate,
get the gist of your ticket –

look here:
in this picture you appear to be figure-skating.
That's Grace on your arm.

Just before –

CLEARED, THEN SET AFRESH

Look: the dawnfringed mousegray
winterquilt of clouds.

*Respectable. Right
where they are.*

We course eastward, my new love and I,
past rust-belt carcasses void-eyed
to the plain bunker of a diner at Razed Corners.

The kind of place you used to frequent:

*trade frissons of recognition with the regular patrons,
disdain thinking 'black' to their 'white',
take your seat, integrate the premises.*

Wished you may, wished you might.

Fast broken, we recognize
how little we know about happiness,
our own in particular.

But you remember:

Children's laughter.
The brooding future? – don't let it trouble you.
You'll profit from it, whatever it brings.

*Give yourself to love and dance while your season's green.
Listen: love's whispers in night's places . . .*

tight counter spaces. The waitress, giggling,
flees a hungry hand.

But you forgot:

*Exchanged the plain and plenty
for ill-considered fancy: indecent proposals,
jumped claims, and dirty deals.*

*So sticky your story you cringe and cry "No!"
watch, helpless, as the bottomless cup drains dry.*

Present where our term is up.
Absent from our new appointment.

Bipolar instability.

That too is being studied, always acuter terminology
contrived. Sooner or later there's bound to be
a breakthrough.

Then the sun will break through.

"Any time, babe," she teases
when I thank her for warming up my cup.

Index of titles / first lines

A neat ring: butts poked into the sand   29
After his ordeal in the wilderness   31
and check into the Afterlife   47
At every station of the cross consider us   32
Cleared, then set afresh   52
Climb to the crater (false pregnancy)   10
"Coffee and tiramisù?"   42
Gospel   27
He's never so light as in light's first flush   29
Heavy sea (recollected in tranquility?)   8
High on his crossbeam, planning his hard next move   33
His shadow crawls across the place of skulls   34
It begins with a crush on Benito   45
Late nude (at the artist's reception)   12
Late nude (suicide over Main Street)   23
Late nude (the seismographer at fault)   7
Late nude (the snapshooter in an attic window)   16
Lately I hear and sense and see extraordinarily   30
My hand rests on my still chest   37
My love was like a middling rose   36
My old love's new wife and I have dined alike   43
Mystery of the standing-butt circle   29
On the prayer queue (what will happen when it rains?)   20
Patient he is in a land of frantic people   27
Picture my switch hoisting the spirited sponge   34
Quit kiss (world without end)   13
Shifting scapes, the stagger of cedars acrest a ridge   28
The break with her and Peter's church (over the phone)   14
The collective fever: he begged it from us   35

Then we'll read solely between the lines   48
Thin ice   50
Tiresias at Fiumicino (love among the ruins)   3
Wayside host (cross words)   17
With hide scraps I shod his feet   35
"You don't know me," I told him   27

About the author

Gregg Friedberg grew up in Columbus, Ohio, but for many years has lived in Upper Sandusky, a rural county seat, and nowadays spends half of each year in Guanajuato, Mexico, where he participates in the bilingual arts-and-culture scene: gives regular readings and is a coeditor of the literary journal *La Presa* published by Embajadoras Press.

Professionally he's been a partner in a computer software company, writing applications for Ohio county government, but has always written poetry, is happiest when writing sequences like *End All & Be All*: loosely, not conventionally narrative, treating a matrix of themes from an evolving perspective.

The Best Seat Not in the House (Main Street Rag, 2010, Embajadoras Press 2017) examines the vexed relationship between Creator and creature, whether God and man or author and protagonist. *Would You Be Made Whole?*, a collection of unruly sonnets, was published in 2015 by Aldrich Press.

The sequence *What's Wrong* (Kelsay Books, 2022) follows the spiritual journey of a (likely superannuated) boy who claims that amidst the awful onslaught of American Marketing he's lost his personal mythmaking faculty: that spontaneous projection of idiosyncratic aspiration onto the world. Does this not sound a promising premise for a collection of lyric poetry?

And Friedberg is completing a collection of photographs with accompanying texts, *The Artist's Reception*, the result of the black-and-white figure photography project he's been working on for the past several years. The texts gradually reveal the history of the speaker and the 'figure' in the photos – their relationship. Selections from the work have appeared in the art magazines *NyghtVision*, *Tagree*, *Noisy Rain*, *tMf*, *Vitruvian Lens*, and *Daydreaming*.

For ten years Friedberg was a member of Frank Bidart's summer workshop at Skidmore College.

Friedberg can be reached at: gefriedberg@gmail.com

In the video recording at the following link, made during one of the monthly readings in Guanajuato, Friedberg presents four sections from *End All & Be All*:

https://www.youtube.com/watch?v=-cbPhzD68kg
(or search: youtube Friedberg November 2018)

www.ingramcontent.com/pod-product-compliance
Lightning Source LLC
Chambersburg PA
CBHW031423040426
42444CB00005B/683